*200 Words to Help You Talk
about Sexuality & Gender*

Laurence King Publishing

200 WORDS

to Help You Talk about

SEXUALITY & GENDER

Kate Sloan

Contents

Gender in Society

Gender Identities

Gender Expression

Biology & Medicine

Stigma & Struggle

Language

Sexual Identities

Romance & Relationships

Friends & Family

Attraction & Desire

Kink
& BDSM

Sexual Behaviour
& Roles

Gender in Society

Gender

A social and cultural identity that can impact how a person behaves, speaks, feels, dresses, is perceived by others, and is treated by people and institutions. Doctors usually label the gender of newborn babies according to their visible genitalia, but some people discover as they grow up that their gender differs from their biological sex. Many people's gender exists somewhere on a spectrum between masculinity and femininity, while some others reject that binary and exist outside it. Many thinkers have argued that gender is an inessential social construct, so we shouldn't necessarily conform to prescribed gendered strictures but should instead create our own unique gender expressions and identities.

Gender Identity

A person's internal sense of their own gender. Importantly, this may differ from the way they express their gender externally with clothes and other aesthetic trappings; it may also differ from the gender other people perceive them as, or the gendered roles they are expected to play in their life. As a result, you can't necessarily tell someone's gender identity just by looking at them. The term 'gender identity' has fallen out of favour with some trans people, who argue that it implies their gender is something they 'identify as', rather than something they simply *are*.

Gender-neutral

Lacking division and specificity related to gender, often for reasons of inclusivity and/or equality. Language can be gender-neutral (such as using they/them pronouns for people of indeterminate gender), as can policies (including paying all employees the same rate for the same work, regardless of gender) and products (such as clothing designed for all bodies and genders), among other things.

Gender Binary

A widespread system of gender classification whereby only two genders are acknowledged: male and female. In many ways, Western culture as a whole is organized around this idea, with gendered roles and attributes being projected on to people based on their assigned sex, and many products and media properties being designated 'for men' or 'for women'. While many people – both transgender and cisgender – feel they fit comfortably into the category of 'man' or 'woman', the gender binary ideology has been heavily criticized for excluding non-binary and intersex people, oversimplifying the ways in which gender can be experienced and expressed, assuming someone's assigned biological sex at birth will always match their gender identity, imposing binaristic gender through colonialism on cultures that don't subscribe to that idea, and creating unnecessary hierarchies of power based on gender.

Gender Spectrum

A continuum between man and woman, or between masculine and feminine, and a more progressive and nuanced view of gender than the gender binary. Some people believe we all contain some kind of interplay between masculine and feminine energies. The concept of the gender spectrum has been criticized for being too linear and thus excluding some non-binary people whose gender exists not *between* maleness and femaleness but rather *outside* those constructs entirely.

Gendered Socialization

The process through which people (especially young people) are taught about the roles and behaviour patterns society expects them to adhere to, based on the gender they were assigned at birth. For example, assigned-female people are often socialized to be passive, considerate and emotionally intuitive, and assigned-male people to be unemotional, aggressive and ambitious. 'Gender essentialists' argue that these traits are inborn, but feminist and trans thinkers have countered that such traits are instead taught and continually reinforced. While some gendered socialization is fairly innocuous, much of it is problematic, harmful and unnecessary, especially since trans and non-binary people usually end up living as a different gender from the one they were socialized as. Some people, such as the trans social psychologist Devon Price, have argued that the idea of gendered socialization is largely oversimplified and that each person is socialized differently depending on their location, culture, parents' views on gender, and so on.

Gender Roles

Societally enforced expectations of how people should look and behave, based on their gender. These roles vary between cultures, and are usually limited to a binary view of gender. In Western culture, for instance, generally men are expected to be strong, assertive and unemotional, and women to be polite, nurturing and passive. Flouting these expectations can have ramifications ranging from mild judgement to social ostracization and even violence. The feminist and trans rights movements have called gender roles unnecessary, restrictive and harmful. As a result, some gendered expectations have changed (for example, it is generally acceptable now for women to work and for men to be stay-at-home fathers), while others have not (assertive women are often still frowned upon in politics and the media, for instance).

Social Construct

It has been widely argued, mostly by feminist and trans thinkers, that society has assigned certain traits, roles, expectations and statuses to specific gender groups, and that these ideas about gender are artificially imposed, rather than being innate. The existence of trans, non-binary and intersex people supports this argument, by making it clear that biological sex and gender expression are two separate things that need not necessarily 'match' in conventional ways. Intersex and non-binary people have also demonstrated that gender and sex are not nearly as simple as the socially constructed binary system would indicate. Some sociological analysis shows that constructing gender categories in this way works to concentrate power into the hands of specific groups of people (in patriarchal societies, men).

Patriarchy

A social system in which men (especially cisgender men) have more power and privilege than any other gender group. This power manifests in countless ways, including men having more wealth and being paid more for equivalent work, men being better represented in politics and media, and men being seen as inherently smarter and more capable than women. Other overarching societal forces, such as white supremacy (systemic racism) and heterocentrism (systemic homophobia), concentrate this power into the hands of cisgender, heterosexual, white men specifically. The feminist movement has critiqued patriarchy for its oppression of women and trans people, and seeks to abolish or overcome it. In many ways, patriarchy harms men too, by holding them to harsh standards of masculinity.

Gender Identities

Woman

An adult female human; a grown-up girl. Feminine gender presentation is common (although not universal) for women. Women can be cisgender (in which case they usually have a vulva and a vagina) or transgender (in which case they may have been born with a penis); there are also non-binary and intersex women (who may have any genitalia). All types of woman are discriminated against in patriarchal societies. Historically women have been largely relegated to roles such as homemaker and childbearer; it is now understood, more widely than ever before, that women can be (and are) much more than that, although reductive stereotypes about them persist.

Man

An adult male human; a grown-up boy. Many have a penis, although some intersex and trans men do not. Many have higher levels of androgens (such as testosterone) in their body than the average woman, although – again – not all do. Many men have a masculine gender presentation, although one can certainly be a man without being masculine (or be masculine without being a man). Men have systemic privilege and power over women in many societies, in that (for instance) they are paid more than women on average for the same work and have an easier time entering fields such as politics, media and science.

Non-binary

A gender identity existing somewhere between the masculine and feminine ends of the gender spectrum, or outside that spectrum entirely. Non-binary people's outward gender expression may be androgynous, but androgyny isn't a prerequisite of being non-binary. Non-binary identities are generally included under the 'transgender' umbrella, and 'non-binary' is often itself considered an umbrella term comprising identities such as genderqueer, agender, bigender and genderfluid. Some non-binary people – although not all – use gender-neutral pronouns such as 'they/them' or 'ze/hir', and gender-neutral appellations such as 'Mx'.

Enby

A phonetic pronunciation of 'N.B.' (non-binary) and an informal term for a non-binary person. It may be used similarly to words such as 'girl/boy' or 'man/woman', as in 'I am attracted to guys, gals and enbies.' It can also be substituted for these words in other terms, such as 'enbyfriend' in lieu of 'boyfriend/girlfriend'. Some non-binary people find the word 'enby' juvenile or silly, so it's best not to assume anyone wants to be called an enby unless they tell you they do.

Cisgender

If someone's internal sense of their own gender (their gender identity) aligns with the sex they were assigned at birth, they are cisgender (often abbreviated to 'cis'). This term comes from the Latin prefix *cis*, meaning 'on the same side of', as opposed to the Latin prefix *trans*, meaning 'on the opposite side of'. Some cis people prickle when described as such, even going so far as to call it a slur, because they're not used to being seen as anything other than the default – but in reality, 'cis' is a factual descriptor as innocuous as 'brunette' or 'British'.

Transgender

If someone's gender identity does not match the gender they were assigned at birth based on their biological sex, they are transgender (often abbreviated to 'trans'). While this might mean they were assigned male and identify as female (or vice versa), 'transgender' is often used as an umbrella term that also encompasses non-binary, intersex, genderfluid and agender people, among others. Some trans people pursue medical treatment, legal reclassification and other methods of bringing their perceived gender into alignment with their gender identity, although one can still be trans without taking these measures. Trans people are widely discriminated against and misunderstood, although the proliferation of trans public figures and the tireless work of transgender rights activists are helping to change that.

Transsexual

Considered an outdated or offensive term by many people, the term 'transsexual' has been largely abandoned in favour of the more modern 'transgender', because being trans is more about gender than sex or sexuality. However, some trans people still prefer to identify as transsexual; the term can denote that one has medically transitioned through hormones and/or surgery, which not all transgender people do. Unless you know for a fact that a particular person identifies as a transsexual, it's usually considered most correct (as with 'transgender') to use this word as an adjective, not a noun, if you use it at all.

Genderqueer

A gender identity word that is sometimes used interchangeably with 'non-binary' and sometimes thought to be its own separate identity. Genderqueer individuals may feel that their gender exists outside the binary, changes from day to day, comprises several different aspects and/or simply can't be described with existing language. Just as to be queer is to deviate from the norms of both heterosexuality and homosexuality, to be genderqueer is to deviate from mainstream gender norms. Genderqueer people may use any pronouns, although many prefer gender-neutral ones. Their gender expression may be androgynous in appearance, but it doesn't have to be.

Genderfluid

Someone whose gender identity and/or gender expression vary over time may identify as genderfluid. A genderfluid person may, for instance, feel like a woman on some days and more androgynous on other days. Some genderfluid people may want to be addressed with different names and pronouns at different times, depending on how they currently feel, gender-wise. Genderfluid people fall under the non-binary umbrella.

Gender-expansive

An umbrella term used to describe people whose gender identities and/or expressions fall outside traditional gender roles and expectations. This may include trans and non-binary people as well as those who feel that their gender can't be adequately described using existing terms.

Agender

An agender person has no sense of having a gender, or has a gender identity that they see as being unknown or undefinable. Agender people fall under the non-binary umbrella, although many non-binary people do have a sense of their own gender and where it exists on (or outside) the gender spectrum, whereas agender people generally understand their gender as being non-existent or undefined. Agender people may use any set of pronouns, including gender-neutral ones, or no pronouns at all.

Two-Spirit

A term used by some North American Indigenous people for a 'third-gender' social and ceremonial role in their cultures. The Indigenous and queer Two-Spirit performer Tony Enos describes Two-Spirit people as having 'both a male and female spirit within them and [being] blessed by their Creator to see life through the eyes of both genders'. Many Indigenous people feel that European colonialism brought homophobia, misogyny and transphobia into their cultures and that complex Indigenous ideas of gender can't be fully understood through the limited viewpoint of the Western gender binary. Two-Spirit is an identity specific to Indigenous people; similar identity words for non-Indigenous people are 'bigender' and 'genderqueer'.

Bigender

A bigender person has two distinct gender identities and/or expressions. These two genders may be male and female, or may be more complex and unusual than those of that binary. Bigender people may fluctuate between their two genders from day to day or moment to moment (similarly to genderfluid people), or they may feel both genders simultaneously within them. Bigender people are considered part of the non-binary and trans communities.

Androgyne

A gender identity that falls under the non-binary umbrella. Androgynes' gender identity may be somewhere between male and female, both at once, oscillating between the two from day to day, or outside that binary altogether. Although some intersex people are androgynes, the two are not synonymous, since gender and biological sex are separate. Androgynes may, but do not always, attire and present themselves androgynously (that is to say, in a gender-ambiguous way).

Omnigender

A gender identity characterized by experiencing oneself as being all genders at once, or cycling through a wide variety of genders; this is sometimes also called 'pangender'. Omnigender people fall under the non-binary umbrella. Their gender presentation may or may not be androgynous, and may change from day to day.

Polygender

Also called 'multigender', 'polygender' is an identity term for people who have several different gender identities. They may experience all these genders simultaneously or they may embody a different gender from day to day. These genders may include male and/or female, or may exist entirely outside that binary. The term is sometimes used interchangeably with 'non-binary' or 'genderfluid'.

Greygender

Short for 'grey agender,' a greygender person exists on the spectrum between having a clear gender and not having one (being agender). This may mean that they are ambivalent about gender, and/or that their sense of their own gender is unclear or intermittent. They may or may not present themselves androgynously.

Demigirl/Demiboy

The prefix *demi*, meaning 'half' or 'partial', is sometimes added to existing gender identities to express the fact that the person being referred to identifies only partially that way. Two of the most common examples are 'demigirl' and 'demiboy', terms used for people who partially identify as a girl or a boy, respectively, regardless of the gender they were assigned at birth. A demigirl may, for instance, feel like a girl only some of the time, feel only partially like a girl, or feel that their gender leans in a 'girl' direction but is not fully embodied by the term 'girl' on its own.

Butch

A gender identity term originating in the lesbian community that usually refers to queer women whose gender expression leans towards the masculine. However, not all butches identify as women (some are non-binary or transmasculine), and not all butches are queer (some are straight). Butch is often seen as the counterpart to femme, although not all butch people date femmes exclusively or at all. The butch/femme dynamic has been criticized by some queer thinkers for replicating heterosexual dynamics in queer relationships, although others have countered that butchness is inherently distinct from maleness and heterosexual masculinity. As with many people who deviate from what is expected of their gender, butches are unfortunately often mocked, stereotyped and discriminated against.

Femme

A gender identity term that usually refers to a feminine-presenting queer woman. People of other genders may also identify as femmes; gay men who identify this way sometimes use the spelling 'fem'. Femmes are often positioned as the counterpart to butches, although not all femmes date butches, and many date other femmes. Some lesbians argue that only lesbian women can identify as femme because butch/femme dynamics are a queer subversion of heterosexual dynamics; however, bisexual women were present in the communities where these terms originated, and have just as much of a right to these terms. Queer femmes may struggle to be 'read as' queer, because their femininity may make them appear straight to other queer people; this is called femme invisibility.

Boi

An alternate spelling of 'boy', this gender identity term may be used by masculine or androgynous queer women, butches, transmasculine people and/ or queer men (among others) to describe their unconventional relationship to masculinity. The term originated in the Black community and is considered part of African American Vernacular English (AAVE), so some people argue that only Black people should identify this way, and that anyone else would be culturally appropriating the term.

Stud

A term originating in the Black lesbian community to describe, predominantly, masculine-presenting queer women. Some people view 'stud' as a Black-specific term for 'butch'. Generally the term is considered culturally appropriative if it is used to identify people who are not Black or Latina/Latino. Someone who feels that their gender identity is somewhere between 'stud' and 'femme' may identify as a 'stem'.

Gender Non-conforming (GNC)

A wide-ranging term for anyone who deviates from traditional expectations about how they 'should' look or act based on the gender they were assigned at birth, or who deviates from strictures of the gender binary more generally. Trans and non-binary people often fall into this category, as do cisgender people whose gender expression defies norms for their gender: for example, men who wear skirts and lipstick, or women with short haircuts who grow out their body hair. The term usually refers specifically to the externally perceptible aspects of gender (appearance, behaviour, manner of speech and so on), rather than the internal, more identity-based aspects. It is sometimes used interchangeably with the terms 'gender-variant' and 'gender-diverse'.

FTM/MTF

Trans men are sometimes referred to as female-to-male (FTM) because they were assigned female at birth and later transitioned so as to live as men; the inverse is true for trans women who were assigned male at birth and transitioned to live as women (male-to-female or MTF). These terms have fallen out of favour with some trans people, who argue that they were always the gender they now live as (for example, a trans man may have always felt like a man even while he was perceived and labelled as a woman pre-transition), making these terms inaccurate to their experience. The terms are also largely associated with people who pursue hormone therapy and sex reassignment surgery, which not all trans people do.

Gender Expression

Gender Presentation

The way a person communicates their gender to the world, through clothing, speech, mannerisms, make-up (or lack thereof), body hair (or lack thereof) and other externally perceptible cues. Also sometimes called 'gender expression'. While a person's gender presentation may give you a clue as to their gender identity, it doesn't necessarily tell the whole story, especially if someone is closeted and/or their gender exists outside easily recognizable, simplistic gender categories.

Gender Performativity

The notion, put forth by the American feminist philosopher Judith Butler in 1988, that gender is something we 'perform' for a 'social audience', using well-established social 'scripts' to help us do so. For example, someone assigned female at birth may go on to wear dresses and lipstick as part of their gender expression, but these trappings are not inherently female; they're just culturally linked with femaleness and thus part of women's expected gender expression in some places and periods. This theory is in many ways foundational to a modern, progressive understanding of gender, because it asserts that a person's biological sex does not automatically imbue them with certain traits (or even certain identities) traditionally associated with that sex, and that our gender identities and expressions need not adhere to the social scripts that have been foisted on us from birth.

Femininity

A collection of traits, roles and behaviours traditionally associated with women and girls. These are socially constructed and thus highly dependent on cultural context; as the French existentialist Simone de Beauvoir put it, 'One is not born, but rather becomes, a woman.' Some manifestations of conventional Western femininity are gentleness, empathy, caregiving, passivity and the colour pink. Definitions of modern femininity are in flux, and attributes such as strength, self-sufficiency and sexual forwardness have become more acceptable for women than they once were. Not all people who appear, behave or identify as feminine are in fact female; people across the gender spectrum can present in feminine ways.

Masculinity

The socially constructed array of traits, behaviours and roles traditionally associated with men and boys. What is considered masculine varies between cultures and periods. Traits such as strength, bravery, assertiveness and sexual initiative are often identified as aspects of modern Western masculinity. Masculinity is not the sole domain of men and boys, since people across the gender spectrum can present themselves in masculine ways and identify as masculine. 'Toxic masculinity' is a specific subset of masculinity norms that harm men and those they interact with; these include misogyny, homophobia, transphobia, the suppression of emotions other than anger, and a propensity for unnecessary aggression.

Transvestite

An outdated term for a cross-dresser (someone who wears clothing made for a different gender than their own). Historically, many people have conflated transvestites with transgender people, because of the low level of public understanding in the past (and even now) that sex and gender are separate, and that the way one dresses doesn't always reflect one's gender identity. The *GLAAD Media Reference Guide* suggests never using the term 'transvestite' unless someone explicitly identifies that way, because of the way it has been used to dismiss, belittle and stigmatize trans and gender non-conforming people for decades.

Cross-dresser

Someone who occasionally or intermittently wears clothes, make-up and/or accessories that were designed for people of a gender different from their own.
This term usually, although not always, describes cisgender men who enjoy wearing clothes designed for women. Cross-dressers' interest in wearing differently gendered clothing may be aesthetic and/or fetishistic, but does not reflect a desire to transition to a different gender or live as that gender full-time, as with trans people. However, some trans people do initially explore their gender through cross-dressing before realizing they are trans or coming out as trans.

Drag Queen/King

Drag queens are typically men (often gay men) who dress up as women for entertainment purposes, including performing onstage or in videos. Likewise, drag kings are typically women (often queer women) who perform while dressed as men. These performances usually invoke exaggerated gender stereotypes in amusing ways.
Drag performers may prefer to be referred to by the appropriate set of pronouns for the gender of the 'character' they play while they're in costume.
While some trans and non-binary people do drag, the two are not synonymous; drag is a performance that occurs only at specific times and in specific settings, while trans people's gender pervades their lives and identities.

Transfeminine

Generally, a transfeminine person is a trans person who was assigned male at birth and has a gender identity somewhere on the feminine-leaning side of the gender spectrum. This includes trans women as well as many feminine-presenting non-binary and intersex people.

Transmasculine

Usually, a transmasculine person is a trans person who was assigned female at birth and now identifies and/or presents in a more masculine-leaning way. This includes trans men as well as some masculine-presenting non-binary and intersex people.

Sissy

Historically often used as an insult towards queer and/or effeminate men, this word has been reclaimed by some people as a gender identity term. Usually a sissy is a person who was assigned male at birth and enjoys behaving and dressing in a feminine way. Sissies may consider themselves trans, non-binary, genderqueer, transfeminine or some combination thereof. Some people, including some cisgender men, like to dress up in traditionally feminine clothes and/or perform traditionally feminine tasks (such as cleaning or cooking) as part of a kinky fantasy, and they may call themselves sissies as well. This term has been criticized for perpetuating the notion that femininity is undesirable and synonymous with weakness; however, some self-identified sissies argue that they are subverting those stereotypes in an empowering way.

Genderfuck

To genderfuck is to 'fuck with gender', to subvert traditional gender roles and expectations, sometimes with the goal of calling attention to the artificiality and mutability of gender. For example, someone can genderfuck their presentation by pairing lipstick with a beard, or wearing sparkly heels with a suit and tie. While it is often used as a verb, a person who messes with gender in this way may also identify as genderfuck(ed), or as a 'gender-bender', a related term. Cis and trans people alike can enjoy experimenting with their gender presentation.

Gender Euphoria

A feeling of joy and comfort that may ensue when a trans person's gender identity is respected and/or they express their gender in a way that feels authentic and empowering. Often considered the opposite of dysphoria, gender euphoria is essentially the pleasure created by concordance between a person's internal sense of their own gender and the way their gender is outwardly expressed or perceived. It can be an important initial indicator for trans people seeking to understand and explore their own gender. For example, a transmasculine person may feel gender euphoria when they bind their breasts or are called 'sir'.

Binding

A practice whereby a person (often a transmasculine person) flattens and conceals their breasts, using some kind of constrictive garment worn under clothing. People who have gender dysphoria related to their breasts may bind as often as daily to alleviate it. Some people also bind for drag performances, cosplay and various other reasons. Commercially produced binders are available, and are safer than DIY options such as wrapping cloth bandages tightly around one's body, which can cause rashes, pain and shortness of breath.

Tucking

The practice of concealing one's penis and testicles from view, often by pulling the penis backwards between the legs while pushing the testicles up into the inguinal canals (the abdominal orifices that testicles descend from during puberty). Specialized underwear-like garments, called gaffs, can be used to keep the penis in place once it's tucked, as can sports tape. Tucking is often done by pre-op or non-op trans women and transfeminine people, to alleviate gender dysphoria and help to prevent them from being misgendered, although it can also be done by cisgender men, drag queens or anyone else who wants to hide their penis temporarily for any reason. If done in the long term, tucking can lower fertility through its effect on testicle temperature, and it may also cause testicular torsion or skin irritation.

Packing

The practice of creating a visible bulge in one's genital region by wearing a dildo, other phallic object or padding in one's underwear. Many pre-op and non-op trans men and transmasculine people pack daily or almost daily, to alleviate gender dysphoria and to be perceived as more masculine. Soft dildos known as packers are available specifically for this purpose, as are 'pack-and-play' dildos, which are flexible enough for packing but firm enough to be used for strap-on sex. Some packers double as stand-to-pee devices (STPs), which have a hole that allows the user to urinate without removing their packer. Packing can sometimes cause skin irritation but is otherwise safe, as long as the packer is cleaned regularly.

Passing

If a trans person is perceived as their correct gender, and is not perceived to be trans, they are 'passing' as cisgender. For example, if a trans woman is perceived by her colleagues to be a cis woman, she 'passes' at work. Passing is a primary goal of medical transition for some trans people, both because it may assuage gender dysphoria and because it can help them to avoid transphobic discrimination, harassment and violence. The goal of passing has been criticized by some for reinforcing the idea that trans people must assimilate into cisnormative society in order to be accepted and granted civil rights. It is also debated whether a non-binary person can 'pass as' non-binary, since the gender binary is still a firmly entrenched doctrine in many societies.

Stealth

A trans person who 'passes' as cisgender, and doesn't tell anyone in their life that they were assigned a different gender at birth, is said to be 'stealth' or 'living in stealth'. Often this requires medical transition, including hormone therapy and gender confirmation surgery. Some trans people are stealth only in specific areas of their lives, such as at work. Trans people who choose to be stealth often do so to avoid the transphobic discrimination, harassment, violence and even criminalization that visibly trans people are frequently subjected to. Some trans people criticize those who live in stealth, arguing that they do so out of shame about being trans; others argue that being stealth is simply living as one's correct gender and so there is nothing inherently shameful or wrong about it.

Biology
& Medicine

Sex

An assortment of physical characteristics, including genitalia, internal reproductive organs, chromosomes and hormone levels, are often said to determine whether a person is female or male. However, biological sex (a physical quality) is distinct from gender (a mental and social identity); in cisgender people, the two match, while in trans and non-binary people, the two are different. Sex isn't as clear-cut as it's often assumed to be, since the factors involved in defining it can vary immensely; a cis woman is still a cis woman even if she's had her uterus surgically removed, for example, and a cis man is still a cis man even if his testosterone levels are low. The concept of sex is further complicated by the existence of intersex conditions such as Klinefelter syndrome and Turner syndrome.

Genitals

The external sex organs: the penis and testicles or the vulva. These play a crucial role in sexual pleasure for most people. While doctors usually assign a baby's legal gender based on what their genitals look like, these body parts don't tell the full story of someone's gender identity *or* biological sex: trans and non-binary people grow up to identify as a different gender from the one they were assigned, and many intersex people have different internal sex organs, hormone levels and/or chromosomes than their external genitals would suggest.

Secondary Sex Characteristics

Physical features of the body that develop during puberty but are not directly related to reproduction, such as pubic hair, facial hair and breasts. These are thought to have evolved to aid with attracting mates, like a lion's mane or a peacock's tail. Intersex conditions, hormone imbalances and hormone blockers can all affect how (or whether) a person develops secondary sex characteristics.

Opposite Sex

The gender-binary paradigm frames the male and female sexes as opposites. This is a limited and not entirely accurate way of looking at sex and gender, for many reasons: trans and non-binary people complicate the idea that there are only two genders, or only one true way to be male or female; intersex people disprove the myth that there are always clear-cut divisions between biological maleness and femaleness; and it has also been argued that constructing men and women as 'opposites' leads to unnecessary division when we are really all more similar than we are different.

Chromosomes

DNA molecules containing genetic material. Human sex chromosomes determine biological sex: usually females have two X chromosomes and males an X and a Y chromosome. Some chromosomal abnormalities are considered intersex conditions, such as Turner syndrome (in which one X chromosome is absent or incomplete) and Klinefelter syndrome (in which an extra X chromosome is present). A person's sex chromosomes cannot be identified by their appearance; a special test called chromosomal karyotyping is required. As with all biological sex determinations, chromosomes do not determine a person's gender, since that is a separate concept from sex.

Intersex

A person born with non-standard variations on, or combinations of, chromosomes, reproductive organs, sex hormones and/or genitals may be considered intersex. There are many different intersex conditions, and it is thought that about 1 in 60 babies is born intersex. Some intersex conditions are noticeable at birth (such as 'ambiguous' genitalia) or at puberty, while some (especially chromosomal irregularities) may not be physically apparent and may require special testing to confirm. Medical interventions to 'normalize' an intersex person's body, including genital reconstruction and hormone treatment, have historically often been forced on intersex people as early as infancy. There is a growing awareness globally that this is a human rights violation, and Malta was the first country to outlaw non-consensual intersex treatment, in 2015.

Dyadic

Non-intersex: having genitals, chromosomes, internal reproductive organs and sex hormone levels that all correspond to a single biological sex (male or female). Dyadic people may be cisgender, non-binary or transgender; their being biologically dyadic has no bearing on their gender identity, since sex and gender are separate. Dyadic people have the privilege of not usually being forced into non-consensual surgery or hormone treatment to 'correct' any 'anomalies' in their sexual biology, something many intersex people are subjected to.

Hermaphrodite

An outdated term, almost always considered offensive, for an intersex person. Specifically, the term usually refers to an intersex person who has both testicular and ovarian tissue (this condition is called ovotesticular disorder). As with intersex people in general, people with this condition are often subject to discrimination, harassment and non-consensual medical intervention to 'fix' their anatomy.

In non-human biology, this term is used to describe organisms that can produce both male and female gametes, such as snails and earthworms.

Medical Transition

The medical process whereby a trans person alters their body to match their gender identity. Medical transition can include hormone therapy and/or various forms of gender confirmation surgery. Not all trans people medically transition in the same ways, or at all. Despite being a life-saving process for many thanks to its role in alleviating gender dysphoria, medical transition is unfortunately inaccessible to many, due to financial, political and/or geographical barriers.

Gender Confirmation Surgery

A surgical procedure (or a series of them) wherein a trans, non-binary or intersex person's body is altered to align with their gender identity – usually alongside hormone therapy, as part of an overall medical transition. This is mainly done to alleviate gender dysphoria and to lessen the chances of being identified as trans and thus targeted for discrimination, harassment and violence. For these reasons, gender confirmation surgery is often literally a life-saving medical intervention. Procedures can include 'top surgery' (breast implants or breast removal surgery), 'bottom surgery' (reconstruction of the genitals), hysterectomy, voice feminization surgery and facial feminization surgery. Not all trans people opt to have surgery, and not all trans people who want or need surgery are able to access it, owing to financial constraints, bureaucratic obstacles in the medical system, social stigma and other factors.

Homologous

Since the same foetal tissue can develop into either a penis or a clitoris depending on hormone levels *in utero*, the penis and the clitoris are homologous structures; that is to say, they share a location and origin but are visually and functionally distinct. This homology is the reason the clitoris, not the vagina, is the pleasure equivalent of the penis for most people with vulvas. Testicles and ovaries are also homologous with one another, as are the scrotum and labia. Intersex people sometimes have atypical combinations of, or variations on, these structures.

Puberty

The hormone-triggered process of physical change that begins around the age of 8–14 as a person's body (typically) becomes capable of sexual reproduction. In people assigned male at birth, this process usually includes the voice deepening, testicles dropping, pubic and facial hair growing, and erection and ejaculation becoming possible. In people assigned female at birth, puberty usually includes breast development, changes in fat distribution, the onset of menstruation and increased growth of body hair. 'Puberty blockers' are a hormone-inhibiting treatment given to some young trans people to prevent the development of physical features that don't 'match' their gender identity and may give them dysphoria. Some trans people describe going through a 'second puberty' later in life, on beginning gender-affirming hormone treatment and learning to live as a different gender.

Hormones

Chemicals secreted into the blood which carry signals that prompt effects such as physical growth, mood swings, hunger, sexual arousal and changes in the reproductive cycle. Usually these are released by endocrine glands, including the thyroid, ovaries and testes. However, sometimes – as in the cases of many transgender people seeking medical transition, and some cisgender people who need or want hormone therapy for medical reasons – artificial hormones are injected or ingested.

Puberty Blockers

Drugs, taken via injection or implant, used to postpone puberty by blocking the release of sex hormones such as testosterone and oestrogen. Puberty blockers are sometimes prescribed to trans and non-binary children to prevent their bodies from going through changes that may trigger dysphoria and lengthen their eventual transition process, should they choose to medically transition. These drugs also offer youth some extra time in which to figure out their gender identity before making decisions about it. Despite transphobic outcry about the supposed damage they cause to youth, the effects of puberty blockers are fully reversible, so if a young person decides they want to go through puberty after all, they can trigger it by simply stopping their blockers regimen.

Hormone Replacement Therapy (HRT)

The administration of artificial hormones. Cisgender people receiving HRT usually do so for medical reasons, such as lessening the side effects of menopause. Trans and non-binary people, on the other hand, usually pursue HRT to bring their body into closer alignment with their gender. Typically, transfeminine people take oestrogens and antiandrogens to prompt effects such as breast development, fat redistribution and slowing growth of body hair, while transmasculine people take androgens to prompt effects such as increased muscle mass, enlargement of the clitoris and a deepened voice. Some of these effects are reversible on stopping treatment, while some are not. HRT can also cause psychological changes, such as mood swings and alteration of libido, which is why some trans people describe the initial stages of hormone treatment as being similar to a 'second puberty'. Not all trans people have access to HRT, for financial and bureaucratic reasons (among others); some acquire and administer their own hormones from sources outside the medical system.

Top Surgery

Surgery often sought out by trans men and other transmasculine people to reduce their chest-related dysphoria and/or to look more conventionally masculine. Top surgery usually involves a bilateral mastectomy (the removal of both breasts) and may also involve contouring the chest so that it looks more like a cisgender man's chest. Potential side effects include scarring and lessened nipple sensation. Barriers to getting top surgery may include finances (since it is expensive and not universally available) and the unreasonably high bars some medical entities set for approving the surgery.

Bottom Surgery

Any of a number of surgical procedures available to alter trans, non-binary and intersex people's genitals and other reproductive organs to align more closely with their gender and thus reduce dysphoria. These include, for transmasculine people, phalloplasty (creating a penis from existing tissue), metoidioplasty (lengthening the clitoris so it resembles a penis) and hysterectomy (removing the uterus), and, for transfeminine people, vaginoplasty (removing the penis and constructing a vagina and vulva in its place). These procedures are invasive and risky, and can be expensive, but many trans people consider them crucial and even life-saving.

While 25–35 per cent of trans people get at least one kind of gender confirmation surgery, less than 15 per cent get bottom surgery, whether because of financial barriers, bureaucratic red tape, social stigma, fear of losing genital sensitivity, satisfaction with one's current genitals, or other factors.

Pre-op

A pre-op trans person is someone who plans to get some form of gender confirmation surgery (usually bottom surgery) but has not done so yet. Typically this means that their genitals are the ones they've had since birth, albeit potentially altered by the effects of hormone therapy. Some pre-op people are uncomfortable with their genitals owing to dysphoria, and may not want them to be touched or looked at during sex. It is generally considered deeply impolite to inquire about a trans person's genitals, surgery status or future surgery plans, just as it would be rude to ask a cisgender person probing questions about their genitals or medical history.

Post-op

A post-op trans person is someone who has had gender confirmation surgery, usually bottom surgery. It takes weeks, sometimes months, of post-operative care for the body to recover from these procedures.

Sex may be drastically different for a trans person after surgery and recovery, owing to their new genital configuration and/or a reduction in dysphoria. Being post-op can also reduce the likelihood of a trans person being identified as trans and thus targeted for harassment and violence.

Non-op

A trans person who chooses not to undergo gender confirmation surgery may identify as non-op. Reasons for this choice may include (but are not limited to) liking one's body the way it is, not experiencing genital dysphoria, concern about losing sensitivity after surgery, being unable or unwilling to spend huge sums of money on surgery, or enjoying being visibly recognizable as trans. Non-op trans people are often discriminated against by the legal system, the medical system and transmedicalists; some jurisdictions even make it impossible for trans people to legally change the gender marker on their IDs without getting surgery first.

Transmedicalism

The belief that experiencing gender dysphoria is a prerequisite for being trans, and that the only way to be a legitimate trans person is to pursue medical transition through hormone therapy and gender confirmation surgery. This viewpoint also emphasizes that all trans people should aim to eventually 'pass' as cisgender. Transmedicalism has been widely criticized by the trans community for many reasons, including that a person can be trans without experiencing dysphoria or adhering to binaristic ideas of gender, and that not all trans people choose to medically transition, nor are they required to in order to be legitimately trans. Transmedicalists who are themselves trans are sometimes derogatorily referred to as 'truscum', a portmanteau meaning 'true transsexual scum', because of the harmful effects of their rhetoric.

The Gay Gene

Many scientists have searched in vain for the singular gene that supposedly makes a person gay. According to current science, several different genes play a role in influencing sexual orientation, including some that are linked to the regulation of sex hormones. Some studies have also found that hormones absorbed by a foetus *in utero* can influence its sexual orientation. The search for the 'gay gene' has inspired much concern and debate in the queer community, owing to the possibility that isolating such a gene would contribute to homophobic discrimination and even open the door to anti-gay eugenicists trying to 'breed out' gay people from society.

Hypersexual

Someone whose libido is deemed unusually high may be diagnosed with hypersexuality. Hypersexual behaviour can be a symptom of certain neurological or psychological disorders, such as Alzheimer's disease or borderline personality disorder. Some drugs also cause hypersexual behaviour. It's hotly debated whether hypersexuality is, itself, a clinical disorder, since definitions of 'normal' libido are highly subjective and depend on context. A similar concept, sex addiction, is also controversial; it's unclear yet whether this is a legitimate addiction in the clinical sense or merely a type of compulsive sexual behaviour.

Hyposexual

Someone whose desire for sex and capacity for sexual arousal are deemed unusually low, and who is distressed by this, may be diagnosed with hyposexuality, or hypoactive sexual desire disorder. While hormonal imbalances and other medical factors can cause hyposexuality, some critics argue that most diagnoses of this disorder are actually just pathologizing asexual people and people whose desire level is lower than average but nonetheless within the realm of normality. Attempts to treat hyposexuality in women with medication have also been criticized for blaming those women's low libidos on their pathology rather than on sociocultural factors, such as relationship problems, the stress of doing inequitable unpaid household labour and the widespread cultural stigmatization of openly sexual women.

Sexual Health

Having a physically, mentally and socially healthy relationship to your sexuality is important for your overall health and well-being. The physical aspects of sexual health may include contraceptive use, genital hygiene, and preventing or treating sexually transmitted infections. On an emotional and social level, being sexually healthy may involve confidently communicating your sexual desires, understanding and respecting the need for consent (both your own and other people's), and maintaining a positive and non-shaming attitude about sex. Sexual health is unfortunately undervalued and not sufficiently covered in sex education programmes or even in many medical schools.

Conversion Therapy

The antiquated, pseudoscientific and homophobic practice of attempting to change someone's sexual orientation from homosexual (or bisexual) to heterosexual, often coercively. It is sometimes administered under the guise of medical legitimacy, but many conversion therapy programmes are run by fundamentalist Christian groups whose homophobia has puritanical, religious roots. Such therapy primarily uses aversive conditioning techniques, such as showing someone gay imagery while they're receiving electric shocks or under the influence of nausea-inducing drugs. Other methods include psychoanalysis and lobotomy. Conversion therapy has been proven totally ineffective; sexual orientation cannot be forcibly changed. It is also widely considered a human rights violation and a form of torture, and is now illegal in many countries.

Ex-gay

People involved in the 'ex-gay movement' attempt to eliminate their same-sex attractions and desires, for religious, moral and/or social reasons, and to help others do the same, using methods such as conversion therapy. Many young people are forced into ex-gay programmes by their homophobic families, although the movement also attracts gay and bisexual adults struggling with internalized homophobia and self-hatred. There is no reliable evidence that sexual orientation can be forcibly changed, and in fact, so many people have defected from the ex-gay movement – including several founders of prominent ex-gay organizations – that an 'ex-ex-gay' movement has formed to oppose it.

Assigned at Birth

Doctors typically look at newborn babies' genitals and declare the baby a girl or a boy based on what they see. However, they're not always right about that designation, since a baby may grow up to have a gender that differs from their biological sex (as with trans people) or their genitals may not accurately represent what their biological sex actually is (as with intersex people). In the LGBTQ+ community, the terms 'AMAB' (assigned male at birth) and 'AFAB' (assigned female at birth) are sometimes used to describe people in a way that differentiates sex assignation from gender identity.

Bioessentialism

The theory that women and men each have inherent, fixed traits associated with their sex, and that this explains differences in their behaviour. Bioessentialism has been widely criticized by feminists and transgender people, on the basis that supposedly gender-specific roles and behaviour are actually taught to, and instilled in, most people from a young age, rather than being innate. Bioessentialists often veer into misogynistic territory by claiming, for example, that women are automatically more suited to domestic labour and less suited to intellectual pursuits than men are; this is another reason this theory has been discredited.

Autogynephilia

Supposedly, a fetish wherein a man finds it sexually arousing to cross-dress or to imagine himself as female. While there certainly are men who find cross-dressing sexually exciting, the purported existence of autogynephilia has often been held up by transphobes as 'proof' that trans women aren't really women, but are merely men with a fetish for self-feminization. Beyond being overtly transphobic, this theory fails to acknowledge the fact that *many* people – including many cisgender people – enjoy feeling attractive in a way that lines up with their gender identity, so of course some trans women become aroused upon seeing themselves attired femininely, in the same way that many cisgender women do.

Stigma & Struggle

Misogyny

The hatred of, contempt towards and/or prejudice against women and girls, because of their gender. Often this extends to anyone who has a feminine-leaning gender presentation or is perceived (whether correctly or not) as being female. Misogyny has been around for millennia, and is a key social force that produces widespread discrimination, such as women being sexually assaulted more often than men, being thought of as fundamentally less rational than men, and being targeted in misogyny-motivated mass shootings. Today the feminist movement continues to fight against misogyny in all its overt and insidious forms, including modern anti-feminist movements that proliferate on the internet.

Misandry

The hatred of, and prejudice against, men and boys. Examples include assuming that all men are sexual predators, or denying men custody of their children in divorce proceedings solely because of their gender. Men's rights activists argue that misandry is widespread, although – to provide just a few counter-examples – studies show that women are sexually assaulted five times more often than men, are paid 17 per cent less than men on average, and are more than twice as likely to be sexually trafficked. Misandry is factually not as dominant a systemic force as misogyny, in the same way that 'reverse racism' against white people is not anywhere near as impactful or common as racism against people of colour. The feminist movement has often been criticized for its 'man-hating' views, although misandry is generally considered a fringe belief within the movement; modern feminism acknowledges inequalities of privilege and power in society and advocates for everyone to have equal rights, freedoms and protections, including men.

Misogynoir

A term coined by the queer Black feminist scholar Dr Moya Bailey to describe the specific blend of misogyny and racism faced by Black women. Harmful stereotypes born of misogynoir include the 'strong Black woman' trope, the belief that Black women are hypersexual, and the view that Black women are inherently more aggressive and angry than other women. Misogynoir also manifests economically: Black women, for instance, are more likely to have lower-paying jobs than their male and/or white counterparts. Misogynoir can be perpetuated by anyone of any gender and race. An intersectional approach, as defined by the Black feminist scholar Kimberlé Crenshaw, is required in order to understand and eradicate the discrimination faced by people who are oppressed on several axes, such as gender and race.

Dysphoria

The psychological distress some trans people feel that results from perceived incongruence between their internal identity and their external appearance. Some trans people may not want certain parts of their body to be looked at or touched, because of the risk of triggering dysphoria. Alleviating dysphoria is a common reason trans people seek out hormone treatment and gender confirmation surgery. While some trans people feel little or no dysphoria, some feel it so intensely that it may prompt self-harm or even suicide, which is one reason gender affirmation treatment is considered a matter of life or death. Gender dysphoria is defined as a medical disorder by the current *Diagnostic and Statistical Manual of Mental Disorders* (published by the American Psychiatric Association), a classification that some trans people feel misunderstands, pathologizes and further stigmatizes transness.

Gender Discrimination

Negatively prejudicial treatment based on gender. This can come in the form of sexism against women, such as paying female employees less than their male counterparts, barring women from having legal control over their own reproductive systems, or portraying women as overemotional and incapable in the media. Gender discrimination also encompasses transphobic discrimination, such as refusing to hire trans people, denying homeless trans people access to shelters, or committing hate crimes against trans people. Gender discrimination has unfortunately been prevalent throughout history, and remains so today.

Gender-based Violence

Physical abuse, sexual abuse, assault and/or murder wherein the victim's gender is a key factor in their being targeted. Usually, the phrase refers to violence perpetrated by men against women and girls, although it can also include violence towards trans and non-binary people. Worldwide, about 1 in 3 women becomes a victim of sexual or physical violence in their lifetime. Trans women, women of colour, disabled women and refugee women are particularly at risk.

Femmephobia

The hatred or disparagement of, and discrimination against, femmes and other feminine-presenting people. This bias is born of systemic misogyny. It can manifest in countless different ways, including the ostracization of femme bisexual women from LGBTQ+ communities for not looking 'queer enough', the denigration and demonization of transgender women, and the ridicule of effeminate gay men. While most femmephobia comes from non-feminine people, feminine people can themselves perpetuate stereotypes and make judgements about their own kind; this is called internalized femmephobia.

Chaser

In the LGBTQ+ community, this term usually refers to a cis person who intentionally dates and/or has sex with mostly or exclusively trans people. Many trans people find it unnerving or offensive to be pursued by chasers, because chasers often fetishize and objectify trans people in ways that feel dehumanizing. However, some trans people *prefer* to date chasers because they enjoy feeling desired and accepted; as the trans writer Kai Cheng Thom puts it, 'I want to resist the idea that [chasers are only ever] fetishizing us – because what does that say about trans folks' bodies? [That] the only way we can be sexy is through fetishization? I don't believe that for a second.' In the queer male community, sometimes the term 'chaser' is short for 'chubby chaser', a man who is attracted to bigger men.

TERF

An acronym of 'trans-exclusionary radical feminist', a particular type of feminist-identifying person who believes that trans people are illegitimate, don't deserve human rights and/or shouldn't be allowed into women's or queer people's spaces or sociopolitical movements. TERFs' transphobic rhetoric actively endangers trans people's lives by contributing to cultural stigma and stereotypes about them, which are a key reason trans people are much more likely to commit suicide or be attacked or murdered than the general population. Many TERF arguments have been scientifically debunked, such as their frequent claim that trans women are sexual predators when statistically trans women are far likelier to be *victims* of sexual assault.

Transmisogyny

The combination of transphobia and misogyny faced by trans women and other transfeminine people. This term was coined by the trans writer Julia Serano in her book *Whipping Girl: A Transsexual Woman on Sexism and the Scapegoating of Femininity* (2007). Some gender theorists have argued that trans femininity can be particularly threatening to men in rigidly binaristic, patriarchal and homophobic cultures, because trans women's existence highlights the mutability of gender and makes some cisgender men question their own sexual orientation. Examples of transmisogyny include the fact that trans women are paid less on average than cis people and trans men, are harassed by the police more often than cis people, and are more likely to be assaulted or murdered. These risks are heightened for Black trans women owing to the intersection of transmisogyny and racism, sometimes referred to as transmisogynoir.

Trans Impostor Syndrome

Many trans and non-binary people experience, at some point, the worry that they 'might not *really* be trans' or might not be 'trans enough' to identify as such. A major contributor to this insecurity is transphobic discourse about 'trans-trenders', people who supposedly identify as trans only because it's cool or trendy. However, given how much discrimination and harassment trans people face, it's doubtful that 'faking' being trans is a widespread practice. The trans journalist Tuck Woodstock argues, 'If you think you're trans, you're trans. If you want to be trans, you're trans.'

Closeted

Someone who has not yet revealed themselves to be gay, bisexual, trans or otherwise non-normative with regards to sex or gender may consider themselves to be 'in the closet', or closeted. There are many reasons a person might choose to stay closeted, whether in specific spaces (such as with family, at work or at church) or in every area of their life. Staying closeted can be a way of staying safe from homophobic or transphobic discrimination or violence. Understandably, higher percentages of the LGBTQ+ population are closeted in places where queerness and transness are highly stigmatized or even criminalized.

Coming Out

Short for 'coming out of the closet', this is the process of disclosing that one is queer or trans (or sometimes kinky or non-monogamous), either on an individual level (such as to one's mother) or on a more public level (on social media, for example). Coming out is often a difficult, emotional experience because of the risk of being judged, ostracized or worse. LGBTQ+ youth are at higher risk of homelessness than straight youth, because their parents may kick them out of the house upon learning they're queer and/or trans. Some people choose to stay closeted or to come out only very selectively, in order to stay safe or avoid unwanted ramifications in their career or social life. While this is often discussed as a one-time thing, in reality most LGBTQ+ people have to come out many times throughout their life, to different people and in different contexts.

Disclosure

It has been hotly debated whether trans people have an ethical obligation to disclose their transness to potential sexual or romantic partners. This is especially a consideration for trans women, particularly trans women of colour, who are often demeaned, attacked or even murdered by straight men to whom they disclose their transness, because of those men's transphobic and homophobic belief that sex with a trans woman is distasteful or would somehow make them gay.

Some trans people choose to be forthcoming about their transness (by mentioning it in their online dating profile, for example) to reduce the likelihood of such events. A trans person who rarely or never discloses their transness is 'stealth'.

Outing

To 'out' someone is to disclose their queerness or transness, either to a specific person or group (such as their family) or publicly (for instance, online). Outing is usually done without the consent of the person being outed. It can be a vindictive act done with harmful intent, and puts the person being outed at higher risk of discrimination, harassment and violence. Some queer activists intentionally 'out' public figures, especially those who hypocritically work against LGBTQ+ rights (such as conservative politicians), because they feel it's the morally correct thing to do. Others feel it is never acceptable to out someone without their permission.

Heteronormativity

The belief that heterosexuality is the default, 'normal' or only legitimate sexual orientation. Heteronormativity exists on both an individual level (as when a newly out bisexual person is told their orientation is 'just a phase') and a systemic level (as with heterosexual couples being represented vastly more often than queer couples in the media). Heteronormativity often has devastating effects for queer people, including reduced access to healthcare that meets their needs, a higher risk of suicidality owing to harassment and discrimination, and fewer of the rights, protections and freedoms that straight people can access without incident.

Hate Crime

A crime – usually a violent attack – in which the perpetrator targets someone who is (or appears to be) a member of a particular marginalized group or demographic that the perpetrator is prejudiced against. Hate crimes can be motivated by misogyny, homophobia, transphobia, racism, antisemitism, xenophobia and many other forms of prejudice. They can also be perpetrated by governments and groups rather than individuals, as with the widespread homophobic murders of gay people by Nazis during World War II. Other examples of hate crimes are the racism-motivated lynching of Black people throughout American history and the homophobia-motivated torture and murder of the gay student Matthew Shepard in Wyoming in 1998.

Homophobia

The hatred or fear of, and discrimination against, people who are (or are perceived to be) gay, lesbian or bisexual. Homophobia exists on both an individual level and a systemic one. Homophobic behaviour ranges from mild 'jokes' to outright violence. Religion, media and conservative political messaging all help to instil and perpetuate homophobia. Research has found that vehement homophobes are more likely to be secretly gay themselves. When an LGBTQ+ person turns their culturally instilled homophobia inwards in the form of self-hatred, anxiety and/or behaviour-policing, they are experiencing 'internalized homophobia'.

Biphobia

The hatred, dismissal and/or fear of bisexuality, and discrimination against bisexual people. Bisexuals are often excluded from both gay and straight spaces for not being 'gay enough' or 'straight enough', told to 'pick a side', accused of faking their sexual orientation 'for attention' or 'just going through a phase', and stereotyped as greedy and promiscuous. Bisexual erasure is a subtype of biphobia wherein a person's bisexuality is ignored or explained away, for instance by calling them straight because they have an opposite-sex partner. Seemingly because of biphobia, bisexuals experience higher rates of suicidality, domestic violence, anxiety, mood disorders and poverty than heterosexuals and homosexuals.

Monosexism

The belief that monosexuality – being attracted to people of only one gender (heterosexuality or homosexuality) – is better or more legitimate than being attracted to people of more than one gender (bisexuality or pansexuality). This belief can manifest as biphobic harassment, discrimination, stereotyping and more. People perpetuating monosexism often tell bisexuals or pansexuals that they should 'pick a side' or be less 'greedy', or that they are actually just gay or straight and pretending to be bisexual for attention. Bisexual/pansexual people who feel shame about their orientation may be experiencing 'internalized monosexism'.

Whorephobia

The stigma and discrimination faced by sex workers, as well as people (usually women) who are perceived as being 'slutty' or 'whorish'. This can range from the false assumption that all sex workers abuse drugs, to the banning of sex workers from online platforms they need in order to earn their living, to the violent attack, rape and murder of sex workers, sometimes by police. The sex workers' rights movement has made some strides in changing the public opinion of sex work, emphasizing its legitimacy as a job like any other, and getting it legalized or decriminalized in some places.

Intersectionality

A theory put forth by Kimberlé Crenshaw in 1989, which posits that the intersections of social identities such as race, gender, sexual orientation and socioeconomic class create unique and layered experiences of oppression and/or privilege. For example, Black women experience different types of stigma and discrimination from those experienced by Black men or white women, albeit with some overlap. The feminist movement has often been rightly criticized for leaving Black women out of the conversation, or even being overtly racist. Adopting an intersectional framework makes social justice movements more inclusive and, ultimately, more effective.

Sexual Abuse

Touching, coercing and/or harassing someone in a sexual manner, without their consent, usually on an ongoing basis. This includes the abuse of adults by other adults, as well as the abuse of children by adults or other children. Because of how broad the definition of sexual abuse is, and how seldom it is reported owing to shame and other factors, it can be difficult to estimate its prevalence. Globally, it is estimated that up to 31 per cent of girls and 17 per cent of boys have been sexually abused, often by family members.

Sexual Assault

Touching someone in a sexual way without their consent, including doing so via coercion or using physical force. This can include anything from unwanted groping to violent rape. Sex with anyone who cannot legally consent (such as children, extremely drunk people or elderly people with dementia) is also classified as sexual assault. Being sexually assaulted can cause post-traumatic stress disorder, depression, social anxiety and other ill effects. It is estimated that 1 in 6 women and 1 in 33 men experience an attempted or completed rape in their lifetime. Some groups – such as trans people, disabled people and asexual people – are at disproportionate risk of experiencing sexual violence owing to their marginalized position in society.

Sexual Harassment

A wide-ranging term for non-consensual sexual attention or touch, including anything from sexual jokes and innuendo to sexual extortion to outright sexual assault. Many prominent sexual harassment cases and laws focus on harassment in the workplace. Often, the perpetrator is in a position of authority over their victim or victims. Since the majority of sexual harassment victims are women, and some victims cope with workplace harassment by avoiding work or quitting their jobs altogether, the prevalence of sexual harassment at work contributes to existing gendered imbalances of power, money and success in many professional fields.

Gatekeeping

The practice of limiting who is allowed into LGBTQ+
spaces and communities and/or denying someone's
LGBTQ+ identity, on the basis of certain people not
being considered 'queer enough' or 'trans enough'
for them to 'count' as part of those communities.
For example, femme bisexual women who mostly
date men may be deemed 'not queer enough' to
go to lesbian parties, asexual people may be told
they're not part of the LGBTQ+ community, and non-
binary people may be accused of not being 'trans
enough' for trans spaces. This behaviour is generally
frowned upon by progressive queer and trans people,
especially since social ostracization from their own
communities can make LGBTQ+ people even more
vulnerable than they already are to discrimination,
violence and suicidality.

Queerbaiting

A technique used by creators of media (especially films
and TV shows) wherein one or more characters are
implied to be queer, in order to capture the attention
of LGBTQ+ viewers, but their queerness is never
confirmed or made explicit. For example, the friendship
between Sherlock and John in the BBC's series *Sherlock*
is often implied to be more intimate than a typical
friendship, although it never expressly turns sexual.
Often, queerbaiting happens because TV networks

and film production studios do not allow overtly queer content and/or do not want to alienate their heterosexual audience. The practice has been criticized by the LGBTQ+ community for using queerness as a marketing tactic, tokenizing queer characters and taking advantage of queer viewers' desire to see themselves reflected in the media they consume while not following through on that promise.

Bisexual Erasure

Throughout history, bisexual people have often had their sexual identity ignored, invalidated or just not perceived by the dominant culture. Many bisexual people are assumed to be either straight or gay, depending on who they're dating at the time; likewise, many bisexual historical figures have been incorrectly chronicled as being heterosexual or homosexual, depending on what historians considered a better or more socially acceptable narrative. This habitual invalidation and historical deletion of bisexuality is known as bisexual erasure, and it's a major way in which bisexuals are disbelieved, rendered invisible and discriminated against to this day.

Compulsory Heterosexuality

The idea that heterosexuality is the assumed default in society, one that everyone is pressured to conform to, in ways both subtle and overt. The term was popularized by the lesbian feminist writer Adrienne Rich, who saw compulsory heterosexuality as a political force that allows men to subjugate women on a systemic level. Manifestations of compulsory heterosexuality in modern society include queer people having to 'come out' because everyone is assumed to be straight by default, queer sexuality being erased and stigmatized, and women being encouraged to romanticize and quest after marriage to men even though heterosexual marriages are sometimes plagued with misogynist mistreatment and household labour inequality.

Cissexism

Prejudice towards, discrimination against and/or exclusion of trans and non-binary people, based on the faulty assumption that everyone is (or should be) cisgender. While not always as violent or overt as transphobia can be, cissexism can manifest in many areas of life. For example, many health organizations omit trans people's existence from their resources, resulting in worse health outcomes for trans people.

Another example of cissexism is binarism, the racist erasure by Western culture of non-binary identities unique to specific cultural groups, such as the Hijra of South Asia, and Two-Spirit Indigenous people.

Cisnormativity

The harmful and incorrect assumption that all people are, or should be, cisgender. Cisnormativity exists both on the individual level (for example, misgendering someone because they don't look the way you assume people of their gender will look) and on the societal level (such as messaging that 'all women should get cervical smears', which ignores the fact that not all women have a cervix and not all cervix-owners are women). Although trans people are only a small segment of the population, their erasure and exclusion are extremely hurtful and have tangible negative effects on their lives.

Language

Neopronouns

Third-person pronouns – often gender-neutral ones, although not always – that are not officially recognized by the language they're a part of. Some of the best-known English neopronouns are 'ze/hir', 'xe/xem' and 'ey/em'. Often these are used by trans or non-binary people who feel that 'standard' pronouns ('she/her', 'he/him', 'they/them') don't fit their gender identity, or who simply prefer neopronouns over other options. Although neopronouns are often regarded as a new phenomenon, some of them have been around for many decades, including the 'Spivak pronouns' ('e/em'), whose first recorded usage was in 1890.

Misgender

To misgender someone is to use language for them, or towards them, that is not in line with their gender – for example, calling a man 'Miss' or using he/him pronouns when referring to a trans woman. This is sometimes done maliciously and sometimes done by accident, but no matter the reason, it can be deeply hurtful and upsetting to the person being misgendered. The trans writer Rose Dommu notes that if you accidentally misgender someone, 'the best way to handle the situation is to apologize, correct yourself and never do it again.'

Deadname

A trans person's deadname is a former name of theirs that they no longer use (often, the one they were assigned at birth), whether they've changed their name legally or just socially. Not all trans people have a deadname, since some don't change their names and/or don't feel strongly about what name(s) they are called, but many do. To 'deadname someone' is to call them by their deadname; as with misgendering, this is sometimes done accidentally and sometimes done out of malice, but is generally considered hurtful and is best avoided. It may even be dangerous to deadname someone since it could 'out' them to onlookers who don't know they're trans.

Mx

Pronounced 'Mix' or 'Mixter', Mx is the gender-neutral equivalent of titles such as Mr, Ms and Mrs. It is used by many non-binary people. Through the work of non-binary activists and advocates, Mx is becoming an available title in more and more settings, such as on passports, driving licenses, healthcare documents and bank forms. However, many countries and institutions still have not acknowledged it as a viable option.

Sexual Identities

Straight

A colloquial term for 'heterosexual' – that is, being a man who is exclusively attracted to women, or a woman who is exclusively attracted to men. Current science shows that about 96 per cent of the population identifies as straight, although studies have also found that approximately 25 per cent of straight women and 12 per cent of straight men have had at least one same-sex encounter. The idea of heterosexuality is less than two centuries old; before that, it was not widely known or accepted that human beings could be classified according to their patterns of attraction.

Gay

Homosexual; attracted primarily or exclusively to people of one's own gender. The word is often associated with homosexual men in particular, although people of other genders can and do also identify as gay. Homosexuality has long been stigmatized and even criminalized in many places, and was falsely designated a mental illness in the *Diagnostic and Statistical Manual of Mental Disorders* until 1973. The gay rights movement has pushed back against systemic homophobia and discrimination towards gay people for decades. Today some people use the word 'gay' as an umbrella term for a range of non-heterosexual identities, similar to 'queer'.

Lesbian

Usually, a woman who is attracted exclusively or predominantly to other women. Other types of person sometimes identify as lesbian, including some non-binary and transmasculine people, often because they align themselves politically or socially with the lesbian community. Lesbians are underrepresented in media compared to gay men, and the depictions that do exist are often hypersexualized or based on homophobic stereotypes.

Bisexual

Attracted to two or more genders, not necessarily in equal measure or in identical ways. While a common misconception holds that being bisexual means being attracted to men and women only, many bisexuals are also attracted to people outside that binary. Current science estimates that 2–3 per cent of the population identifies as bisexual. Bisexuals face unique problems not usually experienced by gay and lesbian people, such as having their sexuality erased or being told to 'pick a side'. Bisexual women are also often sexually objectified or assumed to really be straight, while bisexual men are highly stigmatized and often assumed to really be gay. As a result of these misconceptions and microaggressions, studies tend to find that bisexuals have overall worse mental health than gay and lesbian people.

Pansexual

Attracted to many different genders, or to people regardless of gender. This term is sometimes thought to be more inclusive of trans and non-binary people than bisexuality. The difference between bisexuality and pansexuality is largely a matter of semantics and self-identification, and some people even consider the terms interchangeable.

Queer

Although it was once used mostly as a homophobic slur against gay people, the word 'queer' has been proudly reclaimed by many in the LGBTQ+ community, who now use it as an umbrella term encompassing all non-heterosexual (and sometimes all non-cisgender) people. Some people identify as queer because they feel that no other sexual or gender identity term fully captures the breadth of their existence. The movement to reclaim 'queer' originally sprang from the observation that many LGBT people were 'assimilating' into traditional, heterocentrist society and accepting its norms and values; the queer community is still more radically leftist than the 'mainstream' gay community to this day. In LGBTQ+ academia, 'queer' is sometimes used as a verb: to 'queer' something is to explore it from a non-heteronormative perspective.

Asexual

Asexual people, who are thought to make up at least 1 per cent of the population, experience little or no sexual attraction. They may still have sex, masturbate, participate in kink and/or pursue romantic relationships, but without the element of sexual attraction. Although it has been frequently stigmatized and pathologized, asexuality is more or less accepted now among experts as a valid sexual orientation like any other, and many include it under the LGBTQ+ umbrella. That said, there is still not nearly enough mainstream awareness or acceptance of asexuality, in part owing to its scant representation in the media.

Sex-repulsed

Some members of the asexual community describe themselves as sex-repulsed or sex-averse, meaning that they find the idea of having sex abhorrent, upsetting and/or uninteresting. Not all asexual people are sex-repulsed; likewise, there are some non-asexual people who are sex-repulsed, that is to say they experience sexual *attraction* but are averse to sex itself, for various reasons. Sex-repulsed people sometimes pursue romantic relationships without sex. Such people are not necessarily anti-sex in general; they just don't enjoy it themselves.

Allosexual

Allosexuality is the opposite of asexuality; anyone who regularly experiences sexual attraction may be considered allosexual. Allosexuals can be straight, gay, bi or any other sexual orientation involving sexual attraction to other people. Much like being cisgender or heterosexual, allosexuality is the assumed default; normalizing the usage of this word can help to lessen the 'othering' of asexual people, so that hopefully asexuality will eventually be accepted by all as a fully valid part of the spectrum of sexuality.

Demisexual

People who are demisexual experience sexual attraction only to those with whom they've formed an emotional connection, whether that be a romantic relationship, a close friendship or another type of intimate bond. Demisexuality is considered part of the asexual spectrum, since it's an orientation marked by less frequent sexual attraction than allosexuals experience. While there is a common misconception that demisexuals are against casual sex in general, demisexuality is not a moral stance – it's a sexual orientation. Like all asexuals, demisexuals may choose to have sex with people they're not attracted to, for fun, pleasure, deepened intimacy and various other reasons, and this does not negate the reality of their orientation.

Greysexual

A shortened form of 'grey-asexual' (sometimes also called 'grey-ace'). A greysexual person exists somewhere on the spectrum between asexual and allosexual, in the way that grey exists between black and white. This may mean they experience sexual attraction only occasionally, weakly, ambiguously, under a limited set of circumstances and/or with a limited number of people. 'Greysexual' is also sometimes considered an umbrella term for all identities between the two ends of the asexual–allosexual spectrum, such as demisexuality. Someone who identifies as being somewhere in between aromantic and alloromantic might likewise identify as greyromantic.

Skoliosexual

A skoliosexual person is attracted only to people who are trans and/or non-binary. It's a controversial label because it can be seen as fetishizing gender divergence, although many people who identify this way are themselves trans or non-binary and may feel most comfortable and safe around others from the trans community. The word's etymology has also been criticized, since its Greek root, *skolio*, means 'crooked', which some say implies that trans people are inherently broken. Some people prefer to use the similar term 'ceterosexual', which applies to non-binary people attracted to others whose genders also fall outside the binary.

Heteroflexible

Someone who sees themselves as predominantly straight, but occasionally has queer sex or experiences queer attraction, may identify as heteroflexible. This identity can be based more on behaviour than attraction; for example, a woman who's attracted only to men, but occasionally has threesomes with her male partner and another woman for the fun and excitement of it, may consider herself heteroflexible. This term is often criticized for minimizing or further stigmatizing bisexuality, since some people who are 'technically' bisexual may identify as heteroflexible to avoid biphobic judgement from others, and some bisexuals whose attractions are not split evenly across gender lines may identify as heteroflexible if they don't feel 'bi enough' to claim that label.

Bicurious

Coined in the 1990s during a period of increased cultural awareness about bisexuality, the term 'bicurious' usually refers to people who are straight-identified but interested in experimenting with same-sex partners. However, sometimes a bisexual person may initially self-identify as bicurious before realizing or admitting that they are bisexual. The bicurious label has been accused of contributing to bisexual erasure and stigma, by insinuating that sexual orientation is a choice;

however, some bisexuals say this criticism is itself a form of bisexual erasure since it suggests that bicurious people are actually straight and should be barred from LGBTQ+ communities.

Sapiosexual

Attraction to intelligent people, and being turned on by intelligence, is sometimes called sapiosexuality. It's been fervently debated whether this is a legitimate sexual orientation rather than just a preference, since not every preference amounts to an orientation and – as the journalist Gretchen Brown puts it – 'aren't we *all* attracted to intelligence?' Sapiosexual people have also been criticized for often upholding conventional, classist definitions of intelligence, and sometimes disparaging people they see as 'not smart enough'.

Autosexual

If you're attracted exclusively to yourself, and/or you prefer masturbation over sex with other people, you may be autosexual. Autosexual people can still be in sexual relationships and may even enjoy pleasuring partners, but masturbation remains their own primary or preferred sexual outlet. Some autosexual people may pursue romantic relationships, while others may be aromantic or autoromantic (romantically orientated only towards themselves). Like asexuality, autosexuality has often been pathologized, stigmatized and misunderstood, in part because it has not yet been widely studied.

Sexual Fluidity

The shifting and changing of one's sexual identity over time is sometimes called sexual fluidity. This fluidity may manifest in a short-term way (such as feeling straight one day and bi the next), or in the long term (feeling bisexual in one's youth and more gay as one ages, for example). The phenomenon is more common among women than among men, possibly because of a mix of biological and sociocultural factors. Sexual orientation is usually fixed, and scientific evidence shows that it is impossible to change it forcibly; sexually fluid people therefore usually do not have control over when or how their orientation will shift.

Questioning

Someone who is unsure of their sexual orientation may identify as questioning, as they search for the identity words that fit them best. This word can also describe someone who simply doesn't feel that any existing sexual orientation terms truly capture the way(s) they experience attraction. Questioning youth are at higher risk of experiencing suicidal thoughts and engaging in risky behaviour (such as alcohol abuse or unprotected sex) than other queer youth, possibly because of the confusion and stigma faced by people without a firm sexual label. The 'questioning' identity is included under the LGBTQ+ umbrella.

LGBTQ+

An acronym and umbrella term that encompasses people who are lesbian, gay, bisexual, transgender, queer and more. The '+' symbolizes a number of other identities that fall under the LGBTQ+ umbrella, such as pansexual, asexual, intersex and Two-Spirit. The term seeks to unite a wide variety of queer people, trans people and people who don't conform to mainstream understandings of 'standard' sexuality or gender. People under the LGBTQ+ umbrella all experience systemic oppression of various kinds for who they are, and many feel that this unites them with others from the group politically and socially, despite the ways their individual life experiences differ. Alternative versions of this acronym include LGBTQIA (lesbian, gay, bisexual, transgender, queer, intersex and asexual) and QUILTBAG (queer and questioning, unsure, intersex, lesbian, transgender and Two-Spirit, bisexual, asexual and aromantic, and gay and genderqueer).

QTPOC

Queer and/or trans people of colour. Anyone who isn't white is a person of colour, including (but not limited to) many people of African, Asian, Indigenous and Latino/Latina descent, as well as multiracial people. Owing to the intersection of systemic racism, homophobia and transphobia, QTPOC experience forms of discrimination and harassment that white queer and trans people do not, such as being sexually objectified and fetishized by potential partners for their race, being outnumbered and ostracized by white people at many LGBTQ+ events, and being assaulted and murdered at higher rates. Some of the most important figures in LGBTQ+ history were/are people of colour, including the trans rights activists Marsha P. Johnson and Sylvia Rivera, and the queer feminist writers Audre Lorde and bell hooks.

Dyke

Originally (and still sometimes) used as a derogatory term for a lesbian, especially an androgynous or masculine-presenting lesbian. However, some lesbians have reclaimed the word, and identify proudly as dykes. As with many such reclaimed slurs, only people who explicitly self-identify that way should be referred to as such, and often they prefer that only people from their own community use the term.

Faggot

An archaic, offensive word for a gay man, or a man perceived to be effeminate or weak. Sometimes the term is used to refer to LGBTQ+ people more broadly. Some queer people have reclaimed this slur and proudly self-identify as faggots, although (as with all reclaimed slurs) one should never assume that a person will want to be referred to as such by others, especially by people outside the queer community.

Men Who Have Sex with Men (MSM)

An umbrella term, often used in sexuality research and sexual health discourse, which encompasses all men who have sex with other men, whether they identify as gay, bisexual, pansexual, queer, straight or something else. This term focuses on sexual behaviour rather than sexual identity, since the former is more relevant in discussions of sexual health, and the two are not always exactly aligned – many straight-identified men enjoy sexual contact with other men. The term 'WSW' (women who have sex with women) is also used, although not as commonly.

Women Loving Women (WLW)

An umbrella term for all women who experience romantic and/or sexual attraction towards other women, including lesbian, bisexual and pansexual women. It is sometimes used interchangeably with Sapphic or queer. The term 'WLW' originated in Black queer communities and is sometimes thought to be an identifier that only Black people should use. A related term for men who are attracted to other men, 'men loving men' (MLM), is also used, but not as commonly.

Romance
& Relationships

Aromantic

Someone who experiences little or no romantic attraction is aromantic. Romantic attraction is the desire to be in a romantic relationship with someone and/or to do romantic things with them, such as cuddling, kissing and having emotionally intimate conversations. Aromantic people may or may not be asexual as well; around 30 per cent of asexual people identify as aromantic. Someone can be aromantic and still have close relationships with others; in most cases they can still experience love, just not romantic love. Aromantics face stigma because of the extreme focus on romantic love in Western culture – think, for example, of the pro-LGBT slogan 'Love is love', which implies that romantic love is what makes us human, an idea that excludes and denigrates aromantic people.

Alloromantic

An alloromantic person is someone who experiences romantic attraction and is therefore not aromantic. Most people are alloromantic. It is possible for alloromantic and aromantic people to happily be in relationships with one another, so long as they communicate openly about their feelings and seek to understand and empathize with one another's differing experiences of intimacy and love.

Demiromantic

If you experience romantic attraction only towards people you already have an emotional connection with, you may be demiromantic. This deep connection may be a platonic friendship, a sexual relationship or any other kind of close bond. While many people take a while to warm up to new partners, demiromantic people specifically do not and *cannot* develop romantic desire outside existing intimate emotional connections. A demiromantic person can be straight, gay, bi, asexual or any other sexual orientation.

T4T

Short for 'trans for trans', T4T is a term used by some trans people to describe their interest in dating and/or having sex with other trans people. For some people, T4T is a relatively fixed identity akin to a sexual orientation; for others, T4T attraction may just be occasional. Many trans people find T4T relationships reassuring and healing because of the mutual understanding trans people may share, compared to the transphobia, confusion and stigmatization they may face when dating cis people.

Monogamous

Someone who has only one sexual and/or romantic partner at a time may consider themselves monogamous. The boundaries of a monogamous relationship should be agreed on by its participants, since one partner may, for instance, consider flirty banter with a friend to be cheating, while the other may not. It is widely debated whether monogamy comes naturally to humans or is merely imposed through sociocultural norms.

Non-monogamous

There are many ways to be non-monogamous, ranging from run-of-the-mill infidelity to more above-board forms of non-monogamy, such as open relationships, swinging and polyamory, in which all participants are aware of and consenting to each other's other relationships. When pursued ethically and healthfully, non-monogamy requires ongoing in-depth communication between partners about boundaries, expectations and feelings, especially since most people in Western culture have been raised with monogamous social scripts that can make non-monogamy emotionally precarious. People who enjoy non-monogamy often do so because it allows them more freedom and autonomy, can be fun and exciting, and doesn't require them to get all their social, emotional and sexual needs met by just one person.

Polyamory

A specific type of non-monogamy, in which participants may form several romantic and sexual relationships at a time – as opposed to some more casual forms of non-monogamy, where participants may remain romantically monogamous while having sex with people other than their partner. The two major types of polyamory are hierarchical, in which you may have one or more 'primary partners' who are prioritized emotionally and logistically over your other partners, and non-hierarchical, in which all partners are viewed and treated as equal. Some polyamorous people feel that polyamory is their inborn romantic orientation, rather than being a choice they make.

Swinging

A couple who are up for having various forms of group sex and non-monogamous sex with other couples (and sometimes singles) may consider themselves swingers. Swinging is a particular type of non-monogamy, and usually involves being sexually non-monogamous while remaining emotionally or romantically monogamous with one's primary partner. When swinging, couples may participate in a 'full swap' (trading partners with another couple and having any kind of sex including intercourse), a 'soft swap' (trading partners for only non-intercourse activities) or other, looser styles of group sex. The swinging community is overall more heterosexual and conventional than some other non-monogamous communities. Swingers' clubs, resorts and parties are common places where swingers meet other swingers for sex and companionship.

Friends
& Family

Ally

Being an ally to a marginalized community means supporting and protecting the people in that community, advocating for their civil rights and fighting back against the oppression and discrimination they face. Straight people can be allies to the queer community, cisgender people can be allies to the transgender community, white people can be allies to people of colour, and so on. Having supportive allies can be immensely helpful for marginalized people, both on an individual level and a systemic one.

Chosen Family

In contrast with biological family or 'family of origin', chosen family is the group of friends, partners and/or mentors whom a person regards as being supportive, loving and reliable in the way that families are traditionally expected to be. Chosen family is important to many LGBTQ+ people because of the stigma, rejection and othering that their biological families may subject them to, especially families who are homophobic and/or religious.

Gayby

Also known as 'queerspawn', 'gayby' is an informal term for the child of a gay or queer person or couple. They may be an adoptive child, or biologically related to one or both parents and conceived via artificial insemination, surrogacy or other means. Many homophobic puritans have argued that LGBTQ+ people shouldn't be able to raise children, either because of their 'immoral' 'lifestyle' or because children 'need both a father and a mother' to develop properly; however, it's scientifically established that children of gay couples perform better academically than children of straight couples, and develop just as well psychologically and socially.

Polycule

In polyamory, a polycule is an interconnected group or network of people in non-monogamous relationships with one another. Not everyone in the polycule needs to be dating every other member for it to be called a polycule; for example, if Ashley and Bill are a married couple who sometimes spend time with Ashley's boyfriend Connor and Bill's girlfriend Danielle, the four of them could be considered a polycule. The term is a portmanteau of 'polyamory' and 'molecule', because each person in a polycule represents an atom bonded with other atoms to form a complete 'molecule'.

Social Transition

As opposed to medical transition, social transition is the interpersonal aspect of a trans person's transition. This may include coming out as trans to friends and family, asking to be referred to by a different name and set of pronouns, and beginning to attire oneself according to one's true gender. Some trans people transition only socially and not medically, whether because of financial constraints or other reasons. Especially early in their transition, a trans person may be 'out' only to certain people or groups, rather than coming out to everyone all at once. Some doctors and medical systems allow trans people to access hormones and gender confirmation surgery only if they have already gone through social transition and 'lived as' their true gender for a certain amount of time.

Trans Elders

The older members of the trans community. Because trans people are at higher risk of being attacked or murdered and committing suicide than the general population owing to systemic transphobia, trans people's average life expectancy is lower. As a result, the wisdom and lived experiences of trans elders are often seen as particularly valuable, partly because of their reduced numbers. This dynamic also causes some trans people as young as 30 (or even younger) to take on a sort of 'elder' status in their community. In some cases, someone who came out or transitioned at a younger age may be viewed as an 'elder' by trans people who are older than them but who transitioned later in life, since the younger person may have more years of experience being trans.

Nibling

A gender-neutral alternative to 'niece' or 'nephew' –
that is, the child of one's sibling. It can be used to refer
to one's sibling's children, of any gender, collectively
('I love all my niblings'), or to a specific person, often a
non-binary person (as in 'My young nibling just came
out as genderqueer'). The word is thought to have been
coined by the linguist Samuel E. Martin in the 1950s.

Queerplatonic

A term, mainly used in the asexual and aromantic
communities, for a type of relationship that is more
emotionally intimate and/or committed than a typical
friendship, but lacks a romantic and/or sexual element.
Queerplatonic relationships, also known as 'romantic
friendships', can be a source of comfort and connection,
and may also serve logistical purposes in much the
same way as long-term relationships or marriages do
for allosexual and alloromantic people. For example,
two asexual and aromantic people may decide to form
a queerplatonic partnership that involves sharing a
home and combining their finances. Queerplatonic
relationships are not typically monogamous, although
they can be.

Squish

A term used most often by asexual and aromantic people, which describes a non-romantic and/or non-sexual 'crush' on someone – that is to say, platonically liking them very much and feeling a strong desire to spend time with them and/or be friends with them.

Attraction & Desire

Sexual Attraction

The feeling of wanting to have sex with someone and/or being sexually aroused by them. This attraction can be based on physical appearance, personality traits, scent and other factors. What is broadly considered sexually attractive is highly culture-dependent and influenced by the media. Sexual attraction is distinct from, and does not always overlap with, romantic attraction. People who never or rarely experience sexual attraction may be on the asexual spectrum.

Sexual Orientation

A pattern of sexual attraction (or lack thereof) that is usually lifelong and unchanging, such as heterosexual, homosexual, bisexual or asexual. Science has not yet established clear determining factors for sexual orientation, but has found overwhelming evidence that one cannot deliberately change one's orientation. It is usually assumed that a person's sexual orientation and romantic orientation will match, but sometimes they differ. A person's sexual orientation does not necessarily determine their sexual *behaviour*, since some people choose to have sex with people they're not sexually attracted to, for various reasons. Many people consider their sexual orientation a defining piece of their identity.

Sexual Preference

This was once the most common euphemism for sexual orientation, but it has now been largely rejected by the queer community and the scientific community because it suggests that sexual orientation is a mere choice or lifestyle, rather than being inborn, lifelong and unchangeable as current science indicates. The term is still used by many conservative politicians and other public figures as a dog whistle for their belief that sexual orientation is a choice and that LGBTQ+ people are immoral. Some people use the phrase 'sexual preference' to describe things they like in bed, such as particular activities or kinks.

Romantic Attraction

The desire to participate in romantic activities with someone (such as kissing, cuddling and going on dates) and/or to be in a romantic relationship with them. Romantic attraction tends to be based more on personality and perceived commonalities than sexual attraction, which is often more physical. Contrary to the maxim 'opposites attract', research shows that similarity of demographic and personality correlates positively with romantic attraction. People who don't experience romantic attraction may be aromantic.

Romantic Orientation

The romantic equivalent of sexual orientation. An aspect of identity that determines what gender(s) one is romantically attracted to and/or the way(s) in which one experiences romantic attraction. For example, if a woman is heteroromantic, that means she's romantically attracted only to men; if she's homoromantic, she's romantically attracted only to women; if she's biromantic, she's romantically attracted to people of two or more genders. Other romantic orientations include those on the aromanticism spectrum, including aromantic and demiromantic. A person's romantic orientation doesn't always match their sexual orientation; for example, if a man is bisexual but heteroromantic, he may be sexually attracted to people across the gender spectrum but interested in forming romantic relationships only with women.

Sexual Arousal

The feeling of being 'turned on', 'horny' or sexually excited. Arousal typically has a physiological component (penile erection, vaginal lubrication, quickening heartbeat and so on) as well as a more emotional or psychological component (the mental desire for sexual stimulation or activity). Arousal can be triggered by erotic stimulation (such as being touched sensually, watching porn or thinking about sex), or may simply happen spontaneously. Arousal can be inhibited by many factors, including stress, hormone levels, medication, medical conditions and alcohol consumption. 'Arousal non-concordance' is a common condition in which one's subjective assessment of one's own arousal doesn't match one's physical arousal.

Sexual Identity

The way one thinks of oneself and defines oneself in relation to sexuality. This can include sexual orientation as well as preferred sexual roles (such as top, bottom, dom, sub), favourite activities (for instance, being an oral sex enthusiast or a bondage fan) and relationship styles (being monogamous or polyamorous, for example). Since sexual identity is a more wide-ranging concept than sexual orientation, it is more common for it to change throughout a person's life, although some people's sexual identity remains fairly fixed. Some sexual identity terms, such as 'sapiosexual' (attraction to intelligence), have been criticized for co-opting the language of sexual orientation to describe what is actually just a sexual preference.

Kinsey Scale

Alfred Kinsey was an American sexologist whose groundbreaking sex research shocked his readers in the 1940s and 1950s. After interviewing thousands of people about their sex lives, he developed a scale to quantify sexual orientation, known as the Kinsey scale. It goes from 0 to 6, with 0 meaning exclusively heterosexual and 6 meaning exclusively homosexual; the numbers in between represent various shades of bisexuality. Kinsey designated asexual people with an 'X' instead of placing them on this scale. Being bisexual himself, he understood sexual orientation as a spectrum rather than a set of discrete identities. He also believed one's position on the scale could change throughout one's life. The scale was revolutionary for its time, when sexuality was thought of as rather static and simple.

Libido

A person's sex drive, or level of desire for sex. Influences that can determine libido include sex hormone levels, stress levels, health conditions, medication, the menstrual cycle, emotional factors, history of trauma, relationship health, intake of alcohol and drugs, and age. When it comes to libido, there is no 'normal'; sexual desire varies enormously from person to person, and throughout a person's life.

Spontaneous Desire

A common narrative about sexual desire and arousal is that it strikes out of the blue, like 'a lightning bolt to the genitals', according to the sex researcher Emily Nagoski. This is largely considered the standard model for how desire works: you suddenly want sex, so you seek it out. Nagoski estimates that 75 per cent of men and 15 per cent of women experience spontaneous desire (the numbers are unknown for people of other genders). Men's power in society, and especially over sex education and porn historically, may partially explain why most people seem to believe that desire works – or should work – in this spontaneous way.

Responsive Desire

The counterpart to spontaneous desire, the concept of responsive desire was popularized by Emily Nagoski in her book *Come as You Are* (2015). In this model, pleasure comes *before* desire. For example, if your partner initiates sex with you but you're not turned on yet, the pleasure of their touch may get you in the mood for sex. Since spontaneous desire is the more widespread notion of how desire works, some people may feel 'broken' for rarely or never experiencing it, when in reality their desire is simply responsive instead. It's thought that about 5 per cent of men and 30 per cent of women have mostly responsive desire.

Crush

To have a crush on someone is to be infatuated with them, in a romantic and/or sexual way (but usually primarily romantically). The object of one's infatuation can be called one's crush. This term is especially associated with young people and with the beginnings of relationships, before being smitten develops into love. In the asexual and aromantic communities, the term 'squish' is sometimes used to describe a platonic crush.

Sapphic

Attraction between women is sometimes called Sapphic attraction, a legacy of the ancient Greek poet Sappho, who is thought to have been bisexual or gay because of the homoerotic content of her poems. The term 'lesbian' also comes from Sappho; it's a reference to the Greek island of Lesbos, where she was born. Some people use 'Sapphic' as an umbrella term for all women who are attracted to other women (whether or not they also experience attraction to other genders), including women who are bisexual, pansexual, lesbian or queer. The term is also often taken to include non-binary people who align themselves with queer women's communities and/or experiences.

Gaydar

A portmanteau of 'gay' and 'radar', gaydar is the supposed phenomenon of being able to intuit the sexual orientation of others, and particularly gay people noticing and identifying other gay people. (Identifying others as bi is likewise sometimes called bi-dar.) In reality, guessing someone's sexual orientation is not a foolproof process, and is usually based on stereotypes about LGBTQ+ people's mannerisms, speech patterns, grooming habits and so on, although there is scientific evidence that gaydar judgements are often accurate. Gaydar is especially important in homophobic and/or straight-dominated settings, where self-identifying openly as gay can be controversial or even dangerous, so more subtle methods are needed to connect with other gay people.

Kink
& BDSM

Kink

An umbrella term for an almost infinite number of non-conventional sexual or sensual activities and interests geared towards erotic and/or emotional gratification. This includes BDSM, sexual fetishism, roleplay and much more. Kink has been pathologized and stigmatized for much of its history. Some studies have found that kinky people have, on average, better mental health than non-kinky people, perhaps owing to their community's emphasis on communication, consent and self-expression. As much as half of the population has tried, or fantasized about, a kinky act at least once. Some people consider their kinkiness to be a hobby or preference, while others see it as part of their sexual orientation. As with sex, some people do kink only with romantic partners, while others are comfortable doing it with friends or even near-strangers. The histories of the kink community and the LGBTQ+ community are closely intertwined, since there is a high degree of overlap between the two populations and both experience sexual marginalization and stigma.

BDSM

A subset of kink that encompasses bondage, discipline, domination, submission, sadism and masochism. These are some of the best-known and most popular kinky interests. As with all kink, consent and communication are of utmost importance when participating in BDSM. Many kinky people like to pre-negotiate all their sessions to establish clear consent, and they may use a 'safeword', a pre-chosen, unusual word that any participant may say if they want the session to end immediately. BDSM has been popularized, in part, by the *Fifty Shades of Grey* novels and films, although they depict a kinky relationship that is often abusive and coercive, rather than being consent-focused as all healthy kinky relationships are.

Vanilla

Someone who is not kinky can be described as 'vanilla', although – especially with many kinky activities gaining mainstream popularity in recent years – this may be more of a spectrum than a binary. 'Vanilla sex' is sex that focuses on 'standard' sex acts, such as oral sex and penetrative intercourse, rather than incorporating kinky elements such as bondage, sadomasochism or power exchange. The term 'vanilla' is sometimes seen as an insulting way to dismiss someone for being too boring or 'basic' sexually, but vanilla sex can be every bit as satisfying, intimate and exciting as kinky sex for those who enjoy it.

Fetish

Fetishes, or paraphilias, constitute a specific subtype of kinks. A kink is a non-standard act, object or body part that turns you on, while a fetish is often defined as a non-standard act, object or body part that you *must* incorporate into sex (or fantasize about) in order to reach orgasm. However, scientific data shows that most fetishists also enjoy sex that doesn't involve their fetish, so this definition may not be quite right. Some people simply define a fetish as a kink that focuses on a particular object or body part, such as corsets or feet, as opposed to focusing on kinky acts or roles. Some fetishists consider their fetish to be their sexual orientation, since gender is a less important factor to them in choosing sexual partners than those partners' willingness to participate in fetish activities.

Pervert

Anyone whose sexual interests and desires deviate from culturally established 'normality' may be deemed a pervert. While this term is often used to describe people whose sexual behaviour is genuinely harmful and immoral, such as paedophiles and rapists, it has also long been used in a derogatory way to describe people who are queer, trans and/or kinky, even though there is nothing inherently immoral or harmful about what they do or who they are. The notion of sexual perversion is highly subjective, and dependent on the place and time in which the term is being used, as well as who is using it. Today some kinky people and people with high sex drives proudly self-identify as perverts, although the term is still generally considered offensive.

Dominant

A dominant (or 'dom') is someone who enjoys directing the action and taking control during kink sessions. Dominance may involve giving sensation rather than receiving it – such as wielding a flogger or wearing a strap-on – but many dominants also like to receive sensation, albeit while remaining in control (for instance, by 'commanding' a partner to give them oral sex). As with many forms of kink, dominance *can* manifest in abusive ways, but good dominants always ensure that their submissives are continually consenting to any and all activities they do together.

Submissive

Submissives (or 'subs') are kinky people who enjoy giving up control to a partner sexually. This may involve following a partner's orders, receiving strong sensations such as pain or pleasure at the hands of their partner, and pleasing their partner both sexually and non-sexually. While there's a common misconception that submissives are subservient doormats, many are strong, self-sufficient people who just happen to prefer playing a submissive role in the bedroom. In many cases, it's the submissive's desires, even more than the dominant's, that shape what happens during a kink session.

Switch

In a kink context, a switch is a person who's happy to be either dominant or submissive, or to give or receive sensation, depending on their mood and the situation. Some switches change their sexual role depending on who they're playing with – for instance, they may feel dominant with one partner and more submissive with another – while some switch roles within relationships or even within sessions. Switches don't necessarily fall directly in the middle of the dominant–submissive spectrum; many lean in one direction or another.

Sexual Behaviour & Roles

Sexual Behaviour

The sexual activities a person participates in, including masturbation. A person's sexual behaviour can differ from what their sexual orientation would indicate it might be. For example, some lesbians have sex with men on occasion. This is primarily because sexual attraction is not the only factor involved in making sex pleasurable or desirable, and also because sexual orientation is often more nuanced than we assume. Some systems of sexual categorization, such as the Kinsey scale, incorporate both attraction and behaviour into their criteria.

Fantasy

An erotic image or scenario that one can think about, usually to evoke arousal or excitement. Fantasies may be, but aren't always, a reflection of one's real-life sexual desires, sexual orientation or gender identity; for many people, fantasy is the first place they explore potential changes in these areas. Fantasy is also an ideal medium for trying things that would be impossible in real life, whether because of physical constraints or just social ones, such as sexual taboos and inhibitions. Common fantasies include group sex, rough or 'forced' sex, public sex and various forms of kinky sex.

Unicorn

In non-monogamous communities, bisexual women who are open to joining couples for a threesome are known as unicorns, owing to their supposed rarity. Seeking out a unicorn to join you and your partner for group sex is known as 'unicorn-hunting', and people who do it are sometimes accused of fetishizing or dehumanizing unicorns by viewing them as sexual objects rather than as people, and by not giving them as much autonomy within the group dynamic as the couple gets. While the term is most often applied to women, unicorns can also be male, non-binary or other genders.

Stone

A term popularized by the trans lesbian writer Leslie Feinberg in her novel *Stone Butch Blues* (1993). A 'stone butch' is typically a masculine-presenting lesbian or transmasculine person who derives their erotic pleasure from pleasuring their partner(s), and prefers not to be touched themselves during sex. This is sometimes, though not always, because of a history of sexual trauma or experiencing gender dysphoria related to one's body. Some people use the phrase 'stone femme' to mean a feminine-presenting lesbian who prefers to only *receive* pleasure while having sex. However, people who are neither butches nor femmes may also identify as stone, meaning they derive pleasure from giving pleasure, not receiving touch.

Abstinence

People who decide not to have sex, often for a limited period, are practising abstinence. This decision may be based on religious beliefs (that sex before marriage is sinful, for instance), personal values (such as the desire not to have sex until 'the right person' comes along), health reasons (for example, waiting until one has access to birth control), self-improvement efforts (such as taking time off from sex and dating while healing from a heartbreak), or any other reason. Definitions of 'abstaining from sex' vary; some abstinent people might avoid only penetrative sex, for instance, while others might avoid sexual activity altogether, including masturbation.

Celibacy

A commitment to sexual abstinence over a long period of time, sometimes one's entire life. It is often associated with religious belief; many clergy members, monks, ascetics and so on are celibate, since many religious strictures posit that having sex is sinful or damaging in some way. This is especially true for gay religious people, whom the Catholic Church (among other religious organizations) encourages to remain celibate to avoid committing the 'sin' of homosexuality. A vow of celibacy often also involves deciding to remain unmarried and to avoid romantic relationships.

Incel

While it was coined by a female blogger writing about loneliness, the term 'incel' – short for 'involuntary celibate' – now mainly refers to an internet-based subculture of (primarily) male virgins who blame their lack of romantic and sexual experience on women, feminism and modern society. Incel ideology centres on a sense of entitlement to sex, misogynist resentment of women for not providing sex on command, anti-feminist sentiment and defeatist self-pity about one's own supposed undesirability. The incel community is widely considered a hate group and a terrorism threat because of its overtly misogynistic (and often racist) ideas, and the numerous mass murders that self-identified incels have committed.

Top

Among queer people, a top is a person who predominantly or exclusively does the penetrating when it comes to sex (particularly anal sex), and is rarely or never penetrated themselves. More generally, and especially in the kink community, a top is someone who gives sensation during a sexual encounter – for example, by spanking, biting or tickling their partner. Some people top only in specific contexts or for specific sessions, while for others, 'top' may be more of a sexual identity, meaning that they prefer to give sensation than to receive it, and they derive pleasure from doing so.

Bottom

In a queer sex context, a bottom is usually someone who prefers to be penetrated than to do the penetrating. This is not necessarily a passive role, and people who are active, enthusiastic receptive partners sometimes identify as 'power bottoms'. In the world of kink, to be a bottom is to receive sensation – for instance, to be flogged, slapped or stepped on – rather than giving it. As with tops, some people see bottoming as an occasional activity they engage in, whereas for others, 'bottom' is a sexual identity that pervades their sex life.

Vers

A 'vers' (short for 'versatile') person is someone who enjoys both topping and bottoming, particularly when it comes to anal sex. The term is mostly used in the gay male community. 'Vers' does not typically refer to the kinky usages of 'top' and 'bottom'; a kinky person who likes both receiving and giving sensation is instead called a switch.

Sex-positive

The sex-positive movement aims to change cultural narratives of sexuality by destigmatizing sex, pushing for widespread sex education and emphasizing that any kind of sex between fully consenting adults is normal, healthy and morally permissible. This attitude flies in the face of conventional religious and philosophical frameworks that view sex (especially queer, kinky, premarital, promiscuous or otherwise non-conventional kinds) as sinful, immoral or unhealthy. A movement of 'sex-critical' feminists has sprung up to counter the sex-positive movement, arguing that increased culture-wide sex-positivity perpetuates the sexual objectification, commodification and coercion faced by women.

Sex Work

The exchange of sexual labour for goods or money. 'Sex work' is an umbrella term encompassing street prostitution, escorting, erotic massage, phone sex, stripping, camming, sugar dating, peepshows, performing in porn and many other activities. This work involves physical skills as well as mental and emotional ones. The term 'sex work' was coined in 1978 by the activist Carol Leigh and is generally preferred over more pejorative terms such as 'prostitution' and 'hooking'. The frequent criminalization and stigmatization of sex work have made it a risky endeavour, and many sex workers have called for full decriminalization so that they can do their jobs safely and without police harassment.

Virgin

A virgin is either someone who hasn't had any kind of sex, or someone who specifically hasn't had vaginal intercourse. Conventional definitions of virginity have long been criticized for excluding queer people, trans people and anyone who cannot have penetrative intercourse because of a medical problem. Women's perceived 'virginity status' has been used as justification for countless violent attacks and murders throughout history, because virginity and morality are linked in many cultures. It is now known that the hymen, long thought to be a marker of virginity, can actually be broken or stretched by numerous non-sexual activities, such as horse-riding and using tampons, making it an inaccurate indicator of virginity status. Some people prefer to say that they 'made their sexual debut', since this term is less rife with historical stigma and inaccurate perceptions than 'losing one's virginity'.

Slut

A pejorative term for a sexually promiscuous person, usually a woman or girl. Although this word originally meant 'a dirty, slovenly, or untidy woman', it has come to be associated with sexual promiscuity instead. Sometimes this insult is thrown at people who aren't even promiscuous but are simply perceived as sexually provocative, 'loose' or immoral in some way. A related term, 'slut-shaming', refers to the sex-negative and often misogynist criticism faced by people who are deemed slutty, including instances when rape is blamed on its victims' supposedly debauched behaviour, such as drinking in bars or wearing short skirts. Many people have proudly reclaimed 'slut' as an empowering descriptor for themselves, but it is still largely considered offensive.

Partner

A wide-ranging term for someone with whom one has an ongoing romantic and/or sexual relationship. A sexual partner can also just be someone you've had sex with. In decades past, using the term 'partner' for one's romantic companion was often perceived as something only queer people did, particularly since marriage equality was (and is) inaccessible for LGBTQ+ people in many places, making 'civil partnership' the de facto queer equivalent of marriage. However, today many people of various sexual orientations and genders use the term 'partner' in various ways.

Lifestyle

The phrase 'the gay lifestyle' has long been a dog whistle for anti-gay conservatives. In stating that they disagree with or disapprove of 'the gay lifestyle', they strongly imply that sexual orientation is a choice, which science has proven it is not. This phrase also implies that queer people lead vastly different lives from straight people, and often evokes homophobic stereotypes about gay people being likelier to have sexually transmitted infections, do drugs, have a lot of casual sex, and so on. To the extent that queer people's lives are different from straight people's, it's often because systemic homophobia has effectively barred queer people from certain areas of 'straight' society. There is also no singular 'gay lifestyle' because gay people, like straight people, are individual human beings who differ enormously from one another. The phrase 'transgender lifestyle' has been used in similar ways, to paint transness as an immoral choice rather than a legitimate identity.

Beard

Particularly in vastly homophobic places and times, some gay people will form a romantic relationship (or *pretend* to do so) with a person of the opposite sex, in order to conceal their homosexuality. This companion is known as a beard, owing to their role in 'disguising' their partner's sexual orientation. The beard may or may not know that they are being used as such, or that their partner is gay. For example, closeted Hollywood actor Rock Hudson famously married interior decorator Phyllis Gates amid rumours that he was about to be outed in a gossip magazine. Sometimes both partners act as each other's beards, as with lesbians marrying gay men so that both can hide their orientation and access the institutional benefits of heterosexual marriage, such as tax advantages, healthcare and social acceptance in conservative straight communities. This practice is known as a lavender marriage.

Gold Star

A lesbian woman who has never had sex with a man may identify as a 'gold-star lesbian'. The identifier 'gold star' is also sometimes used by gay men who have never had sex with a woman. This term has been widely criticized for delegitimizing the gayness of people who *have* had sex with someone of the opposite sex (since behaviour and identity are not synonymous), further stigmatizing bisexuality, excluding trans and non-binary people, centring men in a definition of women's sexuality, and making some rape victims feel as though having been raped by a person of the opposite sex somehow negates their gayness.

Eroticism

While the idea of eroticism is often linked to sexual arousal and sexual desire, eroticism can be viewed more broadly to include all bodily pleasures, both sexual and sensual. These pleasures can be anything from touching a soft velvet garment to walking in the rain to watching an exciting movie. Some spiritual traditions, such as Tantra and Karezza, emphasize the more sensual aspects of sexuality as pathways to bliss or transcendence.

LAURENCE KING

Published by Laurence King Publishing
an imprint of The Orion Publishing Group Ltd
Carmelite House, 50 Victoria Embankment
London EC4Y 0DZ

An Hachette UK Company

www.laurenceking.com
www.orionbooks.co.uk

A catalogue record for this book is available
from the British Library.

ISBN: 978-0-85782-950-4

Design: Alex Wright

Origination by F1 Colour, London
Printed in Italy by Printer Trento S.r.l.

Laurence King Publishing is committed to
ethical and sustainable production. We are
proud participants in the Book Chain Project®.
bookchainproject.com